Where Is the Giant?

Written by Jill Eggleton
Illustrated by Philip Webb

PEARSON

The kids are looking for
the giant.

"We can not see the
giant," said the kids.

The kids looked under
the trees.
"Where are you, Giant?"
they shouted.

"The giant is not here,"
said the kids.

The kids looked under
the bridge.
"Where are you, Giant?"
they shouted.

"The giant is not here,"
said the kids.

The kids looked under
the rock.
"Where are you, Giant?"
they shouted.

"The giant is not here,"
said the kids.

The kids went up a hill.

"This is a big hill,"
said the kids.

The kids jumped up
and down on the hill.

"Where are you, Giant?"
shouted the kids.

"Here I am," said the giant.

A Story Map

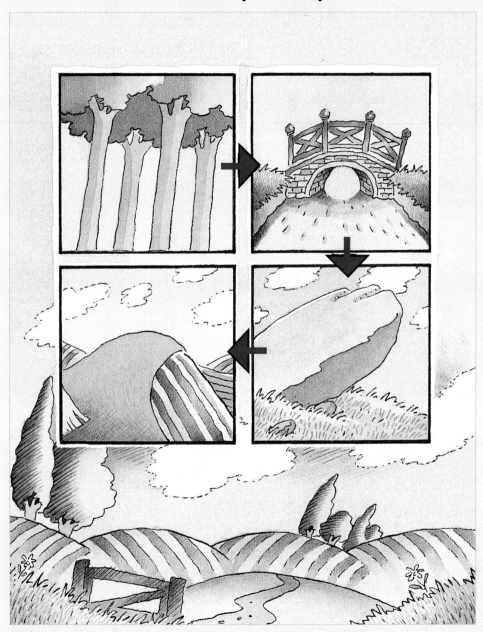

▬▬ Guide Notes

Title: Where Is the Giant?
Stage: Early (1) – Red

Genre: Fiction
Approach: Guided Reading
Processes: Thinking Critically, Exploring Language, Processing Information
Written and Visual Focus: Story Map, Speech Bubbles
Word Count: 112

THINKING CRITICALLY
(sample questions)
- What do you think this story could be about?
- Look at the title and read it to the children.
- Why do you think the children are looking for the giant?
- What do you think about the kids looking under the trees and under the rock for the giant?
- Why do you think the kids could not see the giant?

EXPLORING LANGUAGE

Terminology
Title, cover, illustrations, author, illustrator

Vocabulary
Interest words: giant, kids, trees, bridge, rock, hill, jumped
High-frequency words: where, shouted
Positional words: under, down, on, up

Print Conventions
Capital letter for sentence beginnings and names (**G**iant), full stops, quotation marks, commas, question marks